Contents

Abstract... ii

I. Introduction.. 1

II. Background 2

    a. Defining Cyber Attacks 3

    b. Current International Standards and the Dilemmas.............................. 3

    c. State Sovereignty 4

    d. During Peacetime or in Conflict? 5

    e. State or Non-State Sponsored Attack 6

    f. Estonia Cyber Attacks, April-May 2007 8

    g. The Blame Game 9

III. Analysis of the Estonia Attacks 10

    a. Attribution... 10

    b. Criminal Act vs. Act of War 11

    c. Non-State Cyber Attacks 13

    d. International Support 14

IV. Findings and Recommendations 15

    a. Findings... 15

    b. Recommendations.. 19

V. Conclusion... 23

Bibliography 27

Abstract

For three weeks in 2007, the Republic of Estonia suffered a crippling cyber attack that left government, political and economic facets of the country helpless. This scenario provides a great template to examine the rights of a cyber attacked state in the context of international law. Estonia's options were limited for numerous reasons including difficulty of attribution, lack of international standards, and the current political environment. Ultimately, unless a cyber attack causes undisputable damage and loss of human life, and it can be traced back to a source with high certainty, it is highly unlikely that a state will conventionally respond in self-defense.

Currently, there are no clear international laws that govern the rights of any sovereign state in the event of a cyber attack absent the direct loss of human life or significant physical damage. The current approach is to take the existing laws and treaties and interpret them to fit the activities in the cyber domain. However, unlike a conventional attack, there are many more factors that blur the line in cyberspace. Attribution is much more difficult because there is limited physical evidence and usually is spread across different sovereign states. Without a common (and agreed upon) definition of what constitutes a cyber attack, how can nations defend themselves without risking the ethical, legal and moral obligations that should reign over states? The fundamental dilemma a state faces is to balance its retaliatory options with the requisite legal justifications if they cannot be confident of the source for the attack.

I. __Introduction__

The cyber domain has changed the way individuals, private industry, and countries do business. This reliance on cyber has also added another dimension in the interrelations between these parties especially when undesirable or hostile circumstances are detected. The relationship between sovereign states can be tested by many aspects including when a state is threatened by an adverse action. These actions are not limited to the traditional economic or physical attacks, but now also to an attack in the cyber domain. Government, military, and legal experts have been extensively studying the effects and legalities of cyber activities on international relations. When provoked in a cyber attack in a peacetime environment, it can be argued that states are unlikely to retaliate unless the damage caused by these attacks pose a risk to the survival of the state. The reasons, in conception, may be easily simplified. But in reality, they are complicated technical problems with real political and international implications. First, cyber attack attribution is too difficult. Second, the current international legal standards make it difficult to categorize a cyber attack as a true act of war justifying an armed response. Lastly, state sponsored cyber attacks are either rare, covert, or clandestinely executed, so the majority of the attributed attacks will likely be found as executed by non-state actors. This makes retaliation more problematic.

A sovereign state has little or no retaliation recourse against a cyber attack in the current international environment. The current international laws and norms have not caught up to the rapidly changing technology that is available both to common citizens and nation states. The international community needs to come together and provide a framework to formulate cyber standards in international law much like the Geneva Conventions did in the early 1900s for armed, physical warfare.

The cyber attacks on the country of Estonia in mid-2007 provide an easy-to-understand case study on the complexities that revolve around the complicated cyber world. This paper examines the issues that Estonia faced and their options. These attacks demonstrated the importance of cyber attack attribution. For months, Estonia publically blamed Russia for these attacks bringing diplomatic relations between the two countries to one of its lowest points in their history.[1] This accusation may have been based more on the political climate at the time rather than on any solid evidence. So what were Estonia's options? Any retaliatory action by Estonia could have proved disastrous as it was later discovered that a 20 year old Estonian citizen was responsible for the attack.[2]

This paper is not a technical assessment of the issues involved in cyber attacks. Instead, the purpose of this paper is to give the reader a broad understanding of the current legal environment and the dilemma that an attacked nation finds itself when attacked in cyberspace.

II. Background

Activities in the cyber domain and its evolution are more difficult to trace and examine when compared to conventional kinetic warfare. The legal discussion of cyber attacks and the difficulties with attribution are not new topics, yet consensus has been difficult because of lack of clarity in the current international laws and norms. For example, in 1999, the United States Naval War College hosted a symposium titled Computer Network Attack and International Law where they brought in numerous scholars and legal experts to discuss many of the legal dilemmas regarding Cyber attacks.[3] The President of the Naval War College at the time, Vice Admiral A.K. Cebrowski, opened the symposium with this question, "[d]oes international law require us to wait until lives are lost or property damaged before we may engage in acts of self-defense?"[4] In the ten years since this symposium, little progress has been made in clarifying many of the issues they discussed. This question still has no clear answer today.

a. Defining Cyber Attacks

The cyber domain is often difficult to comprehend because it is intangible by nature. Where a conventional kinetic attack is tangible, a cyber attack is mysterious. It is easy to see the damage of a missile or terrorist bombing. It is easy to tell that an attack has occurred. A cyber attack is different. A basic definition summarizes a cyber attack as "using malicious computer code to disrupt computer processing, or steal data."[5] In addition, the terms cybercrime and cyberterrorism are often associated with cyber attacks, but these labels are difficult to assign because the identity of the attackers, their intent, and their political motivations, if any, are unclear.[6] Also, the term "information operations" or "information warfare" are also associated when talking about cyber attacks. In reality, cyber attacks are only a subset of information operations. Information operations may include the electronic warfare, computer network operations, psychological operations, military deception and operations security.[7] This paper will focus on the cyber attack in general and will not focus on specific kinds of cyber attacks.

b. Current International Standards and the Dilemmas

The United Nations (UN) Charter is the most referenced starting point to this discussion because it outlines internationally recognized standards of behavior between sovereign nations. Specifically, Article 2(4) states, "[a]ll Members shall refrain in their international relations from the *threat or use of force* against the territorial integrity or political independence of any state, or in any other manner inconsistent with the Purposes of the United Nations [emphasis added]."[8] Additionally, Article 39 allows the UN Security Council to "determine the existence of any threat to the peace, breach of the peace, or act of aggression" and decide on measures to deal with such actions.[9] Lastly, the UN recognizes the concept of self defense in Article 51. It states, "[n]othing in the present Charter shall impair the inherent right of individual or collective self defense if an armed attack occurs against a Member of the United Nation."[10] As the most established international governing body, the UN charter is the prevailing international rule set since 1945. These provisions lead to further scrutiny when applied to the cyber domain.

Is a cyber attack different from a conventional attack? Thomas C. Wingfield, an expert on cyber issues and international law,[11] argues how the UN articles should be applied to cyber attacks. He concludes that only the self defense article could be the "sole lawful basis for the use of force under international law" in retaliation for a cyber attack.[12] Additionally, he dismisses the applicability of Articles 2(4) and 39 because of the very distinctiveness of cyberspace and the "clandestine nature of actions."[13] The wording of Article 51 also leads to debate. A state's right to self defense, according to the Charter, can only be invoked after an "armed attack." By using this term, it becomes more restrictive compared to the phrasing in Article 2(4) where states are only forbidden from the "use of force."[14] This phrasing only adds to the confusion as the difference between the use of force and an armed attack generate multiple interpretations that states can use to decide on retaliation options.

c. State Sovereignty

The concept of sovereignty cannot be ignored in the discussion. State sovereignty allows each state to have rights to govern and make decisions as they choose. It allows states to have the legal right to declare war and resort to forcible actions that may not be considered "war" in what Dr. Delibasis describes in three categories: reprisals, self-defense, and collection of contract debts.[15] He describes reprisals as the use of limited force that "under normal conditions would constitute a breach of international law however, they are instead considered as lawful due to the fact that they are relied upon by a given State as the means of remedying an injury inflicted in peacetime."[16] He describes self defense as being a similar action to a reprisal but in a defensive nature instead of retaliatory.[17] Lastly, he notes that his last category for use of limited force as a sovereign right, the collection of contract debts, as being outlawed by the Hague Convention of 1907 except in the case where a state refuses arbitration, prevents the settlement at arbitration, or refuses to pay.[18] Regardless, this third category is not one that provokes discussion with regard to cyber actions. It is often reprisal and self defense that provides the legal right of the state to retaliate in less than full warfare against an action like a cyber attack.

In addition, sovereignty in the context of the cyber domain becomes much more difficult to define. In ancient warfare, territorial boundaries defined a state's area of sovereignty. Boundary disputes and aggressive actions across a state's borders were obvious signs of violations of the concept of sovereignty. It would be easy to define self defense actions. The technical nature of cyberspace makes it different than the accepted domains of land, sea, and air. Here the very nature of the shared cyber domain makes it difficult to correctly establish a boundary whether logically or physically. Actions taken in the cyber domain usually cross multiple physical boundaries but are difficult to detect and trace.

d. During Peacetime or in Conflict?

It is important to note the differences in situational context if the cyber attacks occur during peacetime or during the course of war or conflicts. This paper focuses on the peacetime scenario, but will briefly discuss the issues related to wartime cyber activities. The Geneva

Conventions of 1949 define the international humanitarian law that hopes to limit the effects of armed conflict.[19] It is questionable how applicable the terms of the Geneva Conventions are to cyber attacks, mainly because the cause of these attacks are hard to attribute. Does a cyber attack against a country's water supply violate the rules of proportionality and cause undue harm to noncombatants? How would cyber attacks be different than the strategic bombing campaigns used during World War II? During times of war, cyber activities become another weapon for a state to use and should be limited in accordance with international humanitarian law.

e. State or Non-State Sponsored Attack

The ease of cyber attacks poses another problem. The low entrance cost of the cyber domain gives non-state actors such as terrorist groups, activists, and thrill-seeking hackers the availability and opportunity to inflict damage that was previously limited to more sophisticated groups. For example, an educated hacker in the comfort of his/her own home 5000 miles away, can theoretically disrupt a country's rail or electrical system. By using malicious code like a virus, worm, or denial of service techniques, the adversary can cause blackouts, disrupt supply rail schedules, or cause rail accidents. The possibilities are overwhelming as most modern systems are interconnected via the network. During World War II, a country would need multiple squadrons of bombers, squadrons of fighters for protection, hundreds of man-hours of intelligence, and several tons of munitions to conventionally cause the same effect as today's hacker. This poses a significant problem because the hacker may not be acting on behalf of any sovereign state. An individual activist operating within the borders of one country can cause havoc in a neighboring ally country. Here attribution becomes the key. As international norms

6

focuses on sovereign states, it has limited jurisdiction and difficulty in policing non-state actors. It becomes a local crime issue and should be handled by local law enforcement.

As mentioned above, the most fundamental problem in cyber attacks is indentifying the offender. One good definition for attribution is to "determin[e] the identity or location of an attacker or an attacker's intermediary."[20] By identifying the attacker's intermediaries, as well as the attacker, valuable information can be gained as to the scope of the attack. The difficulty with attribution usually stems from the attacker's deception. Most cyber attacks are masked through different routes and computers in the network often without the real owner's knowledge. The speed at which a cyber attack occurs often causes major issues with attribution. Most victims do not know they are the subject of cyber attacks until significant damage has already been done. The first step a state must face is to confirm that it has been attacked in cyber space. As technology evolves, so does an attacker's techniques and the tools they use. New vulnerabilities are constantly being exploited as software companies roll out new software to consumers. Secondly, the state should determine the extent to which they were attacked and with what techniques. States are always on the defensive when it comes to figuring out an attacker's mode of operation. Time, man-hours, and technical expertise are a few of the costs that a state endures when trying to stop and assess an attack. The majority of states may not be able to afford or do not have the technical knowledge to solve this problem. Finally, it needs to use technical tools to trace the attacker's paths and the host computers used, which could range from the thousands to the millions. As mentioned earlier, this paper limits it discussion of the technical details of the cyber attack attribution. The main point here is that presently governments, industry, law enforcement, and military organizations continue to battle this growing problem of attribution.

f. Estonia Cyber Attacks, April-May 2007

Between April 26 and May 10, 2007, Estonia's data networks experienced greater than normal traffic which hampered daily operations of government, industry, educational, and Estonian daily business.[21] Estonia is a country far ahead of most in the modern world when it comes to embracing the digital technology to enhance the lives of its citizens. Estonians use the Internet to vote, file their taxes, shop and even pay their parking.[22] Therefore, this anomaly in network traffic had a catastrophic effect on the operations of the entire country.

Specifically, the attacks were categorized as distributed denial of service attacks.[23] These types of attacks overwhelm existing networking equipment by flooding the infrastructure with so many network transactions that it eventually cripples the system. In Estonia's case, websites operated by the Estonian government, political parties, banks, media outlets, and various other companies were targeted causing significant disruption to normal business and government operations. For example, government websites that normally processed 1,000 visits a day, were overwhelmed by over 2,000 visits every second.[24] With two-thirds of Estonia's population having access to the Internet via broadband, the effects were significant.[25]

Estonia's financial means were threatened as well. Estonia quickly took damage control measures primarily by blocking network traffic from foreign sources.[26] Its second largest bank, SEB Eesti Uhispank, had to restrict access to their online banking services to network traffic inside Estonia's borders in order to prevent a total crash of its system.[27]

g. **The Blame Game**

After initial analysis of these cyber attacks, Estonia officials pointed the finger at Russia claiming it was a state sponsored attack. The Estonian Foreign Minister, Urmas Paet, stated, "[w]hen there are attacks coming from official IP addresses of Russian Authorities and they are attacking not only our websites but our mobile phone network and our rescue service network, then it is already very dangerous ... The largest part of these attacks are coming from Russia and from official servers of the authorities of Russia."[28] Estonian officials made these serious accusations during a time of tense Estonia and Russia relations. The timing of these cyber attacks coincided with an Estonian action to move the Bronze Soldier Soviet war memorial in the Estonian capital of Talinn. The Memorial commemorated the Russian World War II soldiers that were killed by the Nazis.[29] Estonians, however, deem the statue as a symbol of the years of Russian occupation.[30] This move provoked a strong emotional response both in Russia and from Russian nationals living in Estonia, including days of the worst riots in the streets of the capital since Estonia declared its independence in 1991.[31]

Following the attacks, Estonia immediately appealed to the international community highlighting the seriousness of the attacks in their country. They requested support from the North Atlantic Treaty Organization (NATO) and the European Union (EU).[32] NATO promptly sent cyber terrorism experts to assist Estonia, but was very careful not to lay the blame on the Russian government.[33] As expected, the Russian government responded quickly denying any state sponsorship of the attacks. Russian ambassador Vladimir Chizhov stated, "[i]f you are implying [the attacks] came from Russia or the Russian government, it's a serious allegation that has to be substantiated. Cyber-space is everywhere. I don't support such behavior, but one has to look at where [the attacks] came from and why."[34]

In January 2008, after months of analysis with the help of international technical experts, Estonia finally convicted an Estonian student, of Russian decent, of causing the month long cyber attacks.[35] He was fined the U.S. equivalent of $1635 while admitting he initiated the attack from his personal computer in protest of the move of the Russian statue.[36] This realization was in stark comparison to accusations seven months earlier against Russia.

III. Analysis of the Estonia Attacks

a. Attribution

The reality that a student living in Estonia and not a Russian state sponsored entity was responsible for the disruptive activities in mid-2007 provides a powerful illustration of the importance and difficulty of attribution in the cyber domain. Completely identifying the identity and location of the attacker is technologically and legally difficult. In a normal crime or attack, there is usually an abundance of physical evidence at the scene. The difficulty for the investigators lies in sifting through the evidence. In the cyber domain, this "physical evidence" is limited and theoretically can be spread around the globe. These attackers are usually intelligent and creative using multiple deception techniques to hide their identity and, at times, any trace that their attack even occurred.

The task Estonia was faced with was not only to identify the source of the attacks, but also prove that Russia had sponsored the attacks. At first, Estonian government officials claimed that the attacks originated from Russia and even cited that some came from Russian government computers.[37] Even if Estonia was able to technically prove the source of the attack was within Russian borders, the predicament then becomes how to prove it was government sponsored. There were potentially drastic consequences to falsely accusing another sovereign state

10

especially one with a significantly larger military capability. A Russian government employee could have been acting independently without the knowledge or sponsorship of senior government officials. Another, more likely, scenario was the random citizen, from Russia for example, who caused the attacks without any affiliation to the government. Estonia did not have any legal ground to stand on in that case.

b. Criminal Act vs. Act of War

The Estonian Defense Ministry questioned the point in which a cyber attack constitutes an act of war. "If a bank or an airport is hit by a missile, it is easy to say it is an act of war. But if the same result is caused by a cyber attack, what do you call that?"[38] When the dust settled in Estonia, there was no coordinated cyber attack sponsored by another sovereign nation against another. Instead it was identified as a criminal act by a resident in Estonia. This case became relatively simple because Estonian law enforcement had the proper jurisdiction to investigate and arrest its own citizen.

But during the months before the technical experts were able to correctly attribute the attacks, Estonia had to choose their response from the entire range of options including political, military, economic, or information operation options. Was Estonia legally permitted to retaliate? What factors did Estonia consider and use to make the case to the international community to justify any retaliation? As Estonia ponders its options, they are forced to consider the difficulties of proper attribution in forming its retaliation options against Russia if they did consider the cyber attacks an act of war. There are three fundamental ways to judge the situation. The first is probably the easiest to understand. More of a quantitative approach, it considers exclusively the ends instead of the means when evaluating if a cyber attack should be considered an act of war.[39]

Simply stated, if the effect of a cyber attack is the same as the effect of a conventional attack, then the two means would be both equally judged an act of war. An electrical power plant can be destroyed by a precision guided munitions, disabled by a Special Forces team, or taken off-line permanently by a massive computer virus. All three means are considered acts of war under this more common sense approach. However, this approach, though easier to comprehend, is considered "out of sync" with the United Nations Charter paradigm discussed before.[40] The attacks on Estonia would not be considered an act of force using this methodology as the effects that Estonia suffered, though causing havoc and inconvenience, did not cause extensive physical damage or loss of life.

The second method follows more the thought process of the framers of the United Nations Charter and looks at the means of attack that matters.[41] More popular with academics, this method looks at only the means of attack and views that only an armed attack, usually by traditional military forces, to constitute a use of force.[42] Obviously, Estonia's situation did not constitute being attacked by an act of force. The principal shortcoming with this train of thought is that it does not take into account the new ways an adversary state can "attack" or disrupt another country's sovereignty. The cyber approach is the obvious example.

The third method uses quantitative factors that, when examined, produces more of a qualitative result.[43] This approach has been accepted within many legal communities and is known as the Schmitt Analysis; it uses seven factors to quantitatively rate the incident to determine if it should be considered an act of war.[44] These seven factors include severity, immediacy, directness, invasiveness, measurability, presumptive legitimacy, and responsibility.[45] A rating would be assigned to each of these factors to determine the severity of the situation. This rating can then be used to qualify the act under the UN articles as an act of war or not. Its proponents argue that the Schmitt Analysis provides a "more academically rigorous evaluation of factors affecting a lawful response to a terrorist attack."[46] In a preliminary application of the Schmitt Analysis to the Estonia attacks, it would seem that none of the seven factors would rate very highly. The total result would, like the previous methods, not warrant an act of force according to the current international standards.

In applying the methods to the Estonia scenario, the cyber attacks would not have constituted an act of war when both qualitatively and quantitatively examined. Fortunately, in Estonia's case, there were no reported cases of physical destruction or loss of life due to the cyber attacks. The outcome becomes clear that a cyber attack needs to be almost catastrophic in nature to be considered an act of force. Only when it is considered a "real" act of force do the international standards permit legitimate retaliation usually under the self-defense clause. In this case Estonia had little cause.

c. Non-State Cyber Attacks

Most malicious cyber activities are directly related to political conflicts especially after physical, conventional attacks.[47] Michael Vatis, director of the Institute for Security Technology Studies as Dartmouth College, studied four "real world" incidents and the aftermath of cyber attacks that followed, and correlated that malicious cyber activity have "concrete political and economic consequences."[48] Incidentally, these activities may not necessarily be state sponsored. Vatis categorizes potential attackers in four categories: terrorist groups, targeted nation-states, terrorist sympathizers and anti-U.S. hackers, and thrill seekers.[49] Though, Vatis focused on cyber activities during an environment of war, the situation that occurred in Estonia has similar characteristics with the political and social turmoil that existed between Estonia and Russia.

However, the convicted Estonian student did not fit any of the four categories cited. Non-state sponsored cyber activities are difficult for sovereign states to contend with during a war environment, but when activities of common citizens include cyber attacks, retribution options become even more difficult to comprehend. It is reduced to a criminal issue left to local or national authorities. However, if the persistence of the attacks continues to originate from a state unwilling to intervene in the attacks, especially if it has been put on notice, the attacked state may have some justification to take a recourse action in self-defense.[50]

d. **International Support**

The political climate plays a large role in determining an attacked state's spectrum of retaliatory options. This statement is true regardless of the type of attack, conventional or non-conventional including cyber attacks. When a country is attacked by a terrorist car bomb, political coup d'état, armor battalion crossing a country's borders, or electrons disrupting a government's communication system, the attacked country will always reach for diplomatic support. Support from other nations brings legitimacy to any retaliatory actions. The terrorists attack on the United States on September 11, 2001 and the Japanese attacks on Pearl Harbor on December 7, 1941 are probably the clearest examples of a country being attacked and gaining the support of other international nations. The legitimacy the United States gained in the international community also garnered military support during those times. The difference between those examples and the cyber attacks seen so far is the scope of the damage and destruction. One can look at attacks in two categories. The first and more common attack "may cause disruption of vital systems leading to widespread inconvenience"[51] with no threat to human life. The second type of attack "directly threaten[s] or appear[s] directly to threaten

14

human life."[52] Unless cyber attacks produce the same scale damage and loss of life, international

support will not be favorable to the extent to take conventional retaliatory actions.

Estonia suffered minor damage during the cyber attacks of 2007. Still, officials at NATO

were sympathetic to Estonia's plight. "This is an operational security issue, something we are

taking very seriously….It goes to the heart of the alliance's modus operandi."[53] Additionally,

the EU supported Estonia by sending technical personnel to the capital. Clearly the severity of

the attacks on Estonia fell in the first type of attack. Jaak Aaviksoo, the Estonian Defense

Minister, acknowledged the ambiguity of the situation in relations to the NATO treaty. "At

present, NATO does not define cyber-attacks as a clear military action. This means that the

provisions of Article V of the North Atlantic Treaty, or, in other words collective self-defense,

will not be automatically extended to the attacked country."[54] He added, "[n]ot a single NATO

defense minister would define a cyber-attack as a clear military action at present."[55] Therefore

Estonia was unlikely to receive any military support from NATO even if it was proven that

Russia had sponsored the attack. The political and legal climate would not have supported it.

Without the international support, Estonia would not have the military or economic advantages

in such a conflict.

IV. Findings and Recommendations

a. Findings

The cyber attacks in Estonia highlighted many points. Many of these issues are still

being debated and will take decades before they can be solved. It is a matter of managing the

problem instead of eliminating it.

Attribution is hard. Unlike a conventional attack or act of violence, cyber attacks do not leave the physical evidence that forensics can easily analyze. Cyber forensics is more complicated. It took Estonia months before they fully understood what had occurred and who caused the damage. An alarming fact was that even with the country's technological prowess, Estonia's still had this much difficulty in making positive attribution despite the help of NATO, US and other experts. All states have a long way to go to improve the technical aspects of cyber attribution.

Additionally, once the state locates the attack's source, determining whether it was a state sponsored attack is more significant. Some factors that could help a state make this determination include the persistence and timing of the attack, the sophistication of the tools, the resources of the attacker, and the target and intended consequences.[56] The result of this analysis is critical in justifying any retaliatory action. Retaliatory actions made without proper substantiation could leave a state with diplomatic conflicts within the international community, especially if it is proven to be erroneous later. Therefore, nations will probably err on the side of caution when weighing their retaliatory options.

It is easy for anyone to engage in malicious cyber activities. The entry costs into the cyber domain are cheap. A computer and an internet connection give an individual power that countries decades ago only dreamed of. Furthermore, the end of the Cold War and the lack of the bi-polar environment have motivated states to increase their cyber capabilities as the potential regional conflict areas grow.[57] Whether it is intelligence gathering or potentially deadly effects, any weaker state, individual, or groups - state sponsored or not- have the power to disrupt sovereign and international politics. If restraint had not been exercised by Estonian officials, regional conflict could have erupted between Russia and Estonia. In the end, the statewide turmoil was caused by an individual, who was not state sponsored, and was only 20 years old. The fact that smaller, less wealthy states along with non-state sponsored groups can easily enter inter this realm of warfare creates complexity on the decision makers to use more restraint. Very similar to a terrorist physical attack, all aspects of the situation need to be addressed and examined before deciding on a course of action.

The current international standards do not address cyber activities. The current international standards that most academic scholars apply to cyber space were written during a time when warfare was essentially a kinetic activity. All actions were tangible and were easier to quantify. Therefore, the application of standards such as the UN Charter leaves a lot of room for interpretation. Whether a cyber attack is an act of war or a criminal activity depends on the view of the person defining it. The state being attacked usually has that right to define the action that has been taken against them, but it is subject to scrutiny by the other international players. States must be careful that they do not overstep their legal bounds in making a quick decisive response. There is a strong need to formalize an acceptable set of international rules to cover the cyberspace domain. The current international norms as applied to the Estonian attacks did not support any assertion of the use of force against Russia.

The political environment matters. This fact is not limited to cyber issues, but in all relations between nations. It is very important to remember when dealing with cyber issues that the ambiguity of the UN Charter and other norms makes cooperation between nations crucial in solving the attribution and retaliation problems. Because cyber activities transcend sovereign borders, cooperation between different state's law enforcement, military and industry is vital because attacks can originate from any internet source. If the political environment is not amicable, then the attacked state has fewer options especially if it is economically and militarily inferior to the accused state.

Additionally, the UN Charter has failed to prevent conflicts despite the threat of retribution with UN approval economically, diplomatically, or militarily. Looking at world history in the last half decade, the Charter has failed to prevent conflict whether between UN members bound by the Charter or by states and non-state actors. Therefore, if cyber attacks *can* be clearly classified as a clear threat of use of force against a sovereign state, the UN rules still are not enough to hold states accountable for their actions. The nature of international politics and the power of the UN is a debate outside the scope of this paper. But the perceived lack of real authority the UN has to hold states to its Charter make it difficult to police states on conventional disputes much less malicious cyber activities.

This is everyone's problem. The attacks in Estonia were accomplished with zombie computers, often called BOTNETs, where unsuspecting owners have their computers infected with a malicious code as far away as the United States and Vietnam.[58] Upon command, the code uses the computer to send internet traffic to certain places. Hundreds or thousands of BOTNETs can work in union to disrupt or overload internet systems like those of Estonia's.[59] The attribution problem is obvious here as these millions of BOTNETs are impossible to track. It becomes everyone's problem because the millions of users that do not protect their computers become an accessory to these attacks.

States with little world power can use the cyber domain and be equally as powerful as the wealthiest, most industrialized states. Those most powerful and wealthiest states will have the most to lose in a successful cyber attack because these states tend to take advantage of the automation and networking of the cyber domain.[60] The United States is the obvious example of the extensive use of cyber in U.S. citizen's everyday lives. But Estonia, when compared relatively, may be observed as even more reliant on the cyber technology. The attacks in 2007 demonstrated that no one is free of the effects of a massive successful cyber attack.

There is little to no deterrence to conducting malicious cyber activities. Again the Estonia situation makes this point very well. The Estonian government was able to convict an individual but the fine was only the US equivalent of $1635 dollars. This example demonstrates that individuals face modest punishment if caught. Furthermore, international laws do not offer any definite punishments for those states that violate the use of force criteria. Again, proving a state's involvement is difficult enough without clear retribution consequences. This makes cyber attacks a very cost effective and low risk option for both individuals and states.

b. Recommendations

The United Nations needs to formally examine the current set of legal standard for their applicability to the cyber domain. The current UN Charter leaves plenty to interpretation. Most notably, the terms "armed attack" and "act of force" in Article 51 and Article 2(4), respectively, are unclear and do not work well when labeling actions in the cyber environment. It would be difficult for a state to justify self defense due to an "armed attack" because the damage a cyber attack causes may not be necessarily obvious. Using the methods described before, the prohibition of the use of force under Article 2(4) is hard to use as justification for any support because malicious cyber activities rarely meet the "act of force" guidelines. If a cyber attack only disrupts information flow or degrades the integrity of information, how does a state classify the damage to its sovereignty? The self-defense principle becomes a difficult justification to use in a retaliatory strike, whether conventional or nonconventional retaliation is used. The

19

international community needs to look at these standards to insure that the rights of both large and small sovereign states are protected because each is vulnerable in the cyber domain, especially those who are reliant on technology.

Governments and industry need to agree on an established standard to handle malicious cyber activities. Because industry develops and maintains most of the infrastructure that comprises the cyber domain, it must be integral to helping create the standards. However, because international boundaries are being crossed in cyber space, industry runs into the same sovereignty issues that governments, law enforcement, and military encounter. Industry has the leading role in developing the technical standards for the protocols, security, and equipment that shapes the cyber domain. Their partnership with governments is critical to helping in the attribution and improving the security aspects of the problem.

Domestic laws need to be more synchronized if attribution is to be more reliable and successful and if penalties are to be more deterrent. This may only be a dream for those trying to solve this cyber problem. For example, "search and seizure of material located in computers located abroad may be viewed by foreign sovereigns as a violation of their territorial sovereignty."[61] Without cooperation of local authorities in the state of the attacker's origins, the attacked state has more difficulty, if not the impossibility of gathering necessary evidence to properly attribute the source of the cyber attacks.

Additionally, if the local domestic law does not outlaw or police malicious cyber activities, especially those affecting foreign states, then an attacked state would have to decide if retaliatory actions are worth the conflict possibly without the support of the original state. For example, in 1999, cyber attacks signified by the name "Moonlight Maze" were discovered against the U.S. Department of Defense servers and networks.[62] The attacks breeched classified

20

networks and were able to acquire sensitive information.[63] Eventually, U.S. federal agencies

were able to attribute the attacks with a degree of certainty to the Russian Academy of Science,

an advanced research organization associated with the Russian military.[64] When requested by

the U.S. government, the Russian Ministry of Justice refused to provide judicial assistance

because they claimed no official Russian involvement in the attacks.[65] Additionally, if a Russian

citizen was responsible, the lack of Russian Federal laws would prevent any punishment for the

attacker.[66] The lack of synergy between domestic laws causes numerous problems if individuals

of foreign nations conduct an attack on another state's soil. Even if it is considered a crime in

one state, it may not be in another.

Following the attacks on September 11th in the United States, governments have taken

steps to increase domestic enforcement and penalties against groups or individuals engaging in

malicious cyber activities. The United States passed the Patriot Act which granted law

enforcement agencies more powers against threats to national security including those who

threaten national security using the cyber domain.[67] Additionally, in 2001, the United Kingdom

updated its Terrorism Act and classified "the use of or threat of action that is designed to

seriously interfere with or seriously disrupt an electronic system" as an act of terrorism.[68] These

changes in domestic laws demonstrate the acknowledgement of the potential severity of

malicious cyber activities. They make it easier to handle these activities from a domestic level,

but there are still legal jurisdiction issues when it comes to activities that originate from other

countries.

Formal agreements between nations are necessary. There are many methods where

states can come together to formalize post cyber attack actions making attribution, prosecution

and prevention easier. Multilateral conventions, bilateral agreements, UN General Assembly resolutions, and "codification" of existing customary international law are some of the ways.[69]

These methods vary in participation and degree of enforcement. However despite many

discussions by many governments, legal experts and cyber experts to arrange some of these

formal agreements, nothing close has come together. First, countries are still trying to

understand the cyber problem and how they can serve their long term goals.[70] Secondly, it is

unclear what type of new laws, restrictions, or agreements are necessary. Until a dramatic or

tragic cyber event occurs where multiple countries are effected and loss of human life or capital

is high, countries will continue to stay with the status quo in terms of international regulation.

However, it is paramount that countries solve this problem because without international

consensus, situations such as Estonia's will continue to brew. The next attacked country may not

exercise as much restraint as Estonia and conventionally attack their perceived attacker

erroneously.

There are agreements that can be used as models to create international conventions and

treaties for the cyber domain. The United Nations Treaties on Outer Space[71] and the Convention

of the Law of the Seas are two such examples. In the 1960s, the space domain was at the

forefront of the world's psyche. The following quote taken from the forward of the United

Nations Treaties and Principles on Outer Space Publication provides an idea of the mindset of

the members of the United Nations at the time.

> As is appropriate to an environment whose nature is so extraordinary, the
> extension of international law to outer space has been gradual and evolutionary—
> commencing with the study of questions relating to legal aspects, proceeding to
> the formulation of principles of a legal nature and, then, incorporating such
> principles in general multilateral treaties.[72]

It can be argued that the cyber domain is similarly extraordinary and that similar principles are

needed to provide guidance that the international community can follow. This would provide a framework for state interaction in the event of a catastrophe caused by cyber activities and involving two or more states.

In addition, the international community can base a cyber domain treaty on aspects from the current Law of the Sea.[73] For example, the 1982 United Nations Convention on law of the Sea provides a good model for settling disputes among states. Specifically, part XI, section 5 of the United Nations Convention on the Law of the Sea outlines the authority, jurisdiction, procedures, and advisory roles that provide a mechanism for states in conflict to use.[74] The cyber and open seas domain have similarities because any state or individual has open access and no one state has ultimate control. Therefore, a similar United Nations cyber convention would need to provide the details and procedures for how states can freely interact and resolve conflicts.

V. Conclusion

It has been almost two years since the attacks on Estonia. When Estonia looks back at the situation they faced, they would see that their options were limited due to the lack of substantial proof that the attacks were Russian sponsored; the severity of the attacks were relatively minimal due to the lack of physical damage and loss of life; and the situation did not meet the international standards for self-defense, retaliatory actions. In addition, if it had been a Russian sponsored attack, it would have been very difficult to prove action and intent. For example, a rogue individual in the Russian government committing the offense would not necessarily represent at state sponsored attack. The Estonia scenario is a stark example of the limitations faced by a state attacked in the cyber domain.

Currently, there are no clear international laws that govern the rights of any sovereign state in the event of a cyber attack absent the direct loss of human life or significant physical damage. The current approach is to take the existing laws and treaties and interpret them to fit the activities in the cyber domain. However, unlike a conventional attack, there are more factors that blur the line in cyberspace. Attribution is more difficult because of the limited physical evidence that may be spread across different sovereign states. Without a common (and agreed upon) definition of what constitutes a cyber attack, how can nations defend themselves without risking the ethical, legal and moral obligations that should reign over states? A state faces the fundamental dilemma to balance its retaliatory options with the requisite legal justifications especially if they cannot be confident of the source for the attack.

The complications grow because anyone can cause "damage" to a nation in cyberspace. First, cyber attacks that are state sponsored are hard to prove. Secondly, the majority of the malicious cyber activities probably originate from individual hackers, terrorist groups or curious minors. The Estonia attacks are examples of this. It is not a matter of if, but when the issues of cyber become so great that countries need to come to agreements to create international legal standards in the cyber domain.

Finally, a cyber attacked state, such as Estonia, contends with the legal, technical and political uncertainties. Unless already in a state of war, cyber attacks will rarely lead to any conventional military retaliation. Increased international cooperation will assist in faster, more accurate attribution. Also, individual states must police their own jurisdictions to assist in controlling malicious cyber activities that spread beyond their borders.

There are examples that the international community can use to pattern acceptable standards for states to follow in the cyber domain. The Outer Space Conventions and the Law of the Seas were written during a time when states had to bring order and standards to the space and maritime domains. The cyber domain presents some of the same challenges similar to when these standards were developed.

Sovereign states have been facing the problem in the cyber domain for a couple of decades, but international consensus has been slow to materialize. Speed of technology, legal concerns, and sovereign state rights all need to be considered. It may take a significant, catastrophic event in cyberspace to demand an international consensus. Hopefully, that event will never occur.

---

[1] Traynor, "Russia accused of unleashing cyber to disable Estonia."

[2] BBC News, "Estonia Fines Man for 'Cyber War.'"

[3] Schmitt and O'Donnell, *International Law Studies*, xi.

[4] Robertson, "Self Defense against Computer Network Attack," 121.

[5] Wilson, *CRS Report for Congress: Botnets, Cybercrime, and Cyberterrorism*, 2.

[6] Ibid., 3.

[7] JP 3-13, *Information Operations*, ix.

[8] United Nations, *Charter of the United Nations*, Article 2, paragraph 4.

[9] United Nations, *Charter of the United Nations*, Article 39.

[10] United Nations, *Charter of the United Nations*, Article 51.

[11] Thomas C. Wingfield is a Fellow with the Potomac Institute since 2003. He is an international lawyer with a specialty in national security law. A former naval officer, he holds a B.A. from Georgia State University, a J.D. and Master of Laws from Georgetown University. He has lectured widely and written extensively on cyber conflict, tyranny and democracy, and lawful uses of force in the war on terror. (From Potomic Institute website, www.potomacinstitute .org)

[12] Wingfield, When is a Cyber Attack an "Armed Attack." 12.

[13] Ibid., 11.

[14] Dinstein. "Computer Network Attacks and Self-Defense," 100.

[15] Delibasis, *Right to National Self-Defense*, 95.

[16] Ibid.

[17] Ibid., 96.

[18] Ibid., 98.

[19] International Committee of the Red Cross. "What is International Humanitarian Law?"

[20] Wheeler and Larson, "Techniques for Cyber Attack Attribution." 1.

[21] Lander and Markoff, "Digital Fears Emerge After Data Siege in Estonia."

[22] Ibid.

[23] Traynor, "Russia accused of unleashing cyber to disable Estonia."

[24] Rhoads, "Cyber Attack Vexex Estonia, Poses Debate"

[25] Ibid.

[26] Davis, "Hackers Take Down the Most Wired Country in Europe."

[27] Haplin, "Estonia accuses Russia of 'waging cyber war.'"

[28] Ibid.

[29] Rhoads, "Cyber Attack Vexex Estonia, Poses Debate"

[30] Haplin, "Estonia accuses Russia of 'waging cyber war.'"

[31] Ibid.

[32] Rhoads, "Cyber Attack Vexex Estonia, Poses Debate."

[33] Traynor, "Russia accused of unleashing cyber to disable Estonia."

[34] Ibid.

[35] United Press International, "Emerging Threats, Protesting student behind Estonia cyberwar."

[36] Ibid.

[37] Haplin, "Estonia accuses Russia of 'waging cyber war.'"

[38] Rhoads, "Cyber Attack Vexex Estonia, Poses Debate"

[39] Wingfield, "An Introduction to Legal Aspects of Operations in Cyberspace," 10.

[40] Michael, et all, "Measured Responses to Cyber Attacks Using Schmitt Analysis," 2.

[41] Schmitt, et all, "Computers and War: The Legal Battlespace,"

[42] Ibid.

[43] Wingfield, "Introduction to Legal Aspects of Operations in Cyberspace," 11.

[44] Ibid.

[45] Michael, et all, "Measured Responses to Cyber Attacks Using Schmitt Analysis," 3.

[46] Ibid.

[47] Vatis. *Cyber Attacks During the War on Terrorism*, 9.

[48] Ibid.

[49] Ibid., 12-14.

[50] Delibasis, *Right to National Self-Defense*, 305.

[51] Murphy, "Computer Network Attacks by Terrorists," 327.

[52] Ibid., 327.

[53] Traynor, "Russia accused of unleashing cyber to disable Estonia."

[54] Ibid.

[55] Ibid.

[56] Delibasis, *Right to National Self-Defense*, 304-305.

[57] Ibid., 8.

[58] Lander and Markoff, "Digital Fears Emerge After Data Siege in Estonia."

[59] Wilson, *CRS Report for Congress: Botnets, Cybercrime, and Cyberterrorism*, 5.

[60] Delibasis, *Right to National Self-Defense*, 7.

[61] Murphy "Computer Network Attacks by Terrorists" 329

[62] Delibasis, *Right to National Self-Defense*, 314.

[63] Ibid., 315.

[64] Ibid.

[65] Ibid.

[66] Ibid.

[67] Armistead, *Information Warfare,* 91-92.

[68] Ibid., 91.

[69] Johnson, "Is It Time for a Treaty on Information Warfare," 450-452.

[70] Ibid., 453.

[71] Dr. Delibasis introduces Outer Space Law as a Law applicable to Information Warfare because space assets may be used during information warfare. This author, however, sees Outer Space Law as an example to model Cyber international treaties.

[72] United Nations, *United Nations Treaties and Principles on Outer Space*, v.

[73] Delibasis, The Right to National Self-Defense," 292.

[74] United Nations. *United Nations Convention on the Law of the Sea*, Part XI, Sec 5.

Bibliography

"A Cyber-riot: Estonia and Russia". *The Economist*. May 12, 2007.

Are, David. *When does a "Hacker: Become an "Attacker."* Fort Leavenworth, KS: School of Advanced Military Studies, U.S. Army Command and General Staff College. 1998.

Armistead, E. Leigh, ed. *Information Warfare*. Washington, D.C.: Potomac Books, Inc. 2007

Background Note: Estonia. United States Department of State. May 2008. http://www.state.gov/r/pa/ei/bgn/5377.htm (accessed on 16 November 2008).

Baltic News Service. "Estonian Minister Details History of Cyber Attacks in Lecture at Baltdefcol." September 8, 2007.

Baltic News Service. "Estonian President Calls for EU Law to Combat Cyber Attacks." March 12, 2008.

BBC News. "Estonia Fines man for 'Cyber war.'" BBC News, 25 January 2008. http://news.bbc.co.uk/2/hi/technology/7208511.stm (accessed 26 Nov 08)

Brenner, Susan W. *Symposium: Technological Change and the Evolution of Criminal Law: "At Light Speed": Attribution and Response to Cybercrime/Terrorism/Warfare.* Chicago, IL: Northwestern University, School of Law. 2007.

Central Intelligence Agency. The World Factbook: Estonia. Last updated 6 November 2008. https://www.cia.gov/library/publications/the-world-factbook/geos/en.html (accessed on 16 November 2008.

Conway, Maura. "Cyberterrorism: Hype and Reality." In *Information Warfare*. Edited by Leigh Armistead. Washington, D.C.: Potomac Books, Inc. 2007.

Davis, Joshua. "Hackers Take Down the Most Wired Country in Europe." *Wired*. 21 Aug 2007. http://www.wired.com/politics/security/magazine/15-09/ff_estonia (accessed 2 April 2009)

Delibasis, Dimitrios. *The Right To National Self-Defense*. Bury St. Edmunds, UK: Arena Books, 2007.

Dinstein, Yoram. "Computer Network Attacks and Self-Defense." In *International Law Studies*, Vol 76, edited by Michael N. Schmitt and Brian T. O'Donnell, 99-119. Newport, RI: Naval War College, 2002.

Dissanayake, Kyrill. "Analysis: Estonia Accuses Russia over Cyber-attacks." *BBC Monitoring Europe*. BBC Worldwide Monitoring. May 17, 2007.

Elder, LtGen Bob. "Cyber Domain Protection and the National Defense." Lecture at NDIA Defense CIP Conference 2008, Miami FL. 8 April 2008. http://www.dtic.mil/ndia/2008dip_cip/Elder.pdf. (Accessed 16 Nov 2008)

Halpin, Tony. "Estonia Accuses Russia of 'Waging Cyber War.'" *The Times*, 17 May 2007. http://www.timesonline.co.uk/tol/news/world/europe/article1802959.ece (accessed 26 January 2009).

Hollis, Duncan B. *Why States Need an International Law for Information Operations.* Portland, OR: Lewis and Clark Law School. 2007.

International Committee of the Red Cross. "What is International Humanitarian Law?" Advisory Service on International Humanitarian Law. July 2004. http://www.ehl.icrc.org/images/resources/pdf/what_is_ihl.pdf

Johnson, Phillip A. "Is It Time for a Treaty on Information Warfare?" In *International Law Studies*, Vol 76, edited by Michael N. Schmitt and Brian T. O'Donnell, 439-455. Newport, RI: Naval War College, 2002.

Joint Publication (JP) 3-13. *Information Operations*, 13 February 2006.

Kelsey, Jeffery T.G. *NOTE: Hacking into International Humanitarian Law: The Principles of Distinction and Neutrality in the Age of Cyber Warfare.* Ann Arbor, MI: Michigan Law Review Association. 2008

Lander, Mark and John Markoff. "Digital Fears Emerge After Data Siege in Estonia." *New York Times*, 29 May 2007. http://www.nytimes.com/2007/05/29/technology/29estonia.html (accessed 20 Jan 2009)

Lok, Joris Janssen. "Cyber-Hostilities; NATO, U.K. launch Cyber-defense Strategies in Wake of Attack on Estonia. *Aviation Week & Space Technology.* Mar 31, 2008.

Michael, James B., Thomas C. Wingfield, and Duminda Wijesekera. "Measured Responses to Cyber Attacks Using Schmitt Analysis: A Case Study of Attack Scenarios for a Software-Intensive System." Proc. Twenty-seventh Annual Int. Computer Software and Applications Conf., IEEE. Dallas TX. November 2003.

Murphy, John F. "Computer Network Attacks by Terrorists: Some Legal Dimensions." In *International Law Studies*, Vol 76, edited by Michael N. Schmitt and Brian T. O'Donnell, 323-351. Newport, RI: Naval War College, 2002.

Rhoads, Christopher. "Cyber Attack Vexes Estonia, Poses Debate." *Wall Street Journal*, 18 May 2007). http://online.wsj.com/public/article/SB117944513189906904-__3K97ags67ztibp8vLGPd70WXE_20070616.html (accessed 17 November 2008).

Robertson, Horace B. Jr. "Self-Defense against Computer Network Attack under International Law." In *International Law Studies*, Vol 76, edited by Michael N. Schmitt and Brian T. O'Donnell, 121-145. Newport, RI: Naval War College, 2002.

Schmitt, Michael N. "Computer Network Attack and the Use of Force in International Law: Thoughts on a Normative Framework." United States Air Force Academy, CO: Institute for Information Technology. June 1999.

Schmitt, Michael N. "International Law and the Use of Force: The Jus ad Bellum." *Connections*, 89-97, September 2003.

Schmitt, Michael N. *Wired warfare: Computer network attack and jus in bello.* International Review of the Red Cross, Vol 84. June 2002.

Schmitt, Michael N., Heather A. Harrison, and Thomas C. Wingfield. *Computers and War: The Legal Battlespace.* Cambridge, MA: International Humanitarian Law Research Initiative, Harvard University. 2004.

Schmitt, Michael N., and Brian T. O'Donnell, eds. *International Law Studies.* Vol 76. New Port, RI: Naval War College. 2002.

Silver, Daniel B. "Computer Network Attack as a Use of Force under Article 2(4) of the United Nations Charter." In *International Law Studies*, Vol 76, edited by Michael N. Schmitt and Brian T. O'Donnell, 73-97. Newport, RI: Naval War College, 2002.

Traynor, Ian. "Russia Accused of Unleashing Cyberwar to Disable Estonia." *The Guardian*, 17 May 2007. http://www.guardian.co.uk/world/2007/may/17/topstories3.russia (accessed 26 January 2009).

United Nations. *Charter of the United Nations.* United Nations Publications. http://www.un.org/aboutun/charter/.

United Nations. *United Nations Convention on the Law of the Sea,* http://www.un.org/Depts/los/convention_agreements/texts/unclos/closindx.htm

United Nations. *United Nations Treaties and Principles on Outer Space.* ST/SPACE/11/Rev.2 United Nations Publication. New York, 2008.

United Press International. "Emerging Threats, Protesting Student Behind Estonia Cyberwar." *United* Press *International,* 28 January 2008. http://www.upi.com/Emerging_Threats/2008/01/28/Protesting_student_behind_Estonia_c yberwar/UPI-57311201570921/ (accessed 26 January 2009)

US Department of Defense, Office of General Counsel. *An Assessment of International Legal Issues in Information Operations.* 2nd ed. August 1999.

Vatis, Michael A. *Cyber Attacks During The War On Terrorism: A Predictive Analysis.* Hanover, NH: Cyber and Dartmouth College, Institute for Security Technology Studies at Dartmouth College, 2001.

Vatis, Michael A. *Cyber Attacks: Protecting America's Security against Digital Threats.* ESDP-2002-04. Cambridge, MA: John F. Kennedy School of Government, Harvard University, June 2002.

Washington, Ollie, Jr. *The Legal and Ethical Implications of Information Operations.* Carlisle Barracks, PA: U.S. Army War College, 2001.

Waterman, Shaun. "Who cyber smacked Estonia?" *United Press International,* 11 June 2007. http://www.upi.com/Security_Industry/2007/06/11/Analysis_Who_cyber_smacked_Estonia/UPI-26831181580439/ (accessed 26 January 2009)

Weber, Amalie M. *Annual Review of Law and Technology: VIII. Foreign & International Law: A Cyberlaw: Cybercrime: The Council of Europe's Convention on Cybercrime.* Berkley CA: Berkeley Technology Law Journal. 2003.

Wheeler, David A., and Gregory N. Larson. *Techniques for Cyber Attribution.* IDA Paper P-3792. Arlington, VA: Institute for Defense Analysis, October 2003.

Wilson, Clay. *CRS Report for Congress: Botnets, Cybercrime, and Cyberterrorism: Vulnerabilities and Policy Issues for Congress.* Order Code RL32114. January 29, 2008.

Wingfield, Thomas C. and James B. Michael. *An Introduction to Legal Aspects of Operations in Cyberspace.* NPS-CS-04-005. Monterey, CA: Naval Postgraduate School. 2004.

Wingfield, Thomas C. *When is a Cyber Attack an "Armed Attack?" : Legal Thresholds for Distinguishing Military Activities in Cyberspace.* The Potomac Institute for Policy Studies. February 2006.